It Takes a Team

Mike Cameron

Mike Cameron
with Greg Brown

TRIUMPH
BOOKS
CHICAGO

Library of Congress Cataloging-in-Publication Data is available upon request.

This book is available in quantity at special discounts for your group or organization.
For further information, contact:
Triumph Books
601 South LaSalle Street
Suite 500
Chicago, Illinois, 60605
(312) 939-3330
Fax (312) 663-3557

Mike Cameron will donate his proceeds from the sale of this book to the Cam4Kids Foundation, a nonprofit organization founded by Mike and his wife, Jabreka, to support programs that benefit children. Mike can be found on the Internet at www.mikecameron.com.

Printed in the United States of America
ISBN 1-57243-502-X
Interior design by Patricia Frey

How To Be a Great Teammate

10. Respect your sport.
9. Respect your coach and teammates.
8. Be coachable.
7. Be accountable.
6. Be positive.
5. Play with passion.
4. Cheer for your teammates.
3. Always give your all.
2. Have fun, but know when to be serious.
1. Think we, not me.

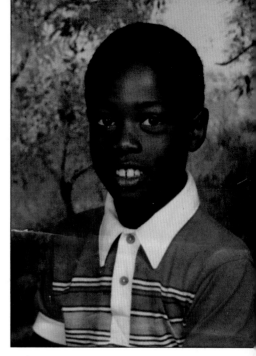

Mike at age seven.

Brian Bahr/Getty Images

How's it going? I'm Mike Cameron, and I'm a professional baseball player. I've played on many teams in my sports career—both successful teams and some that weren't so hot.

Along the way, I've learned what makes a group a team. And I've picked up tips on how to be a positive teammate from many people, including two of the greatest athletes of my generation. I've written this book to help you be a team player in whatever you decide to do.

While not everyone can be a superstar, everyone can be a great teammate.

The Mojo That Matters

Some people believe that grabbing a lot of money is the most important thing in the world. Some believe you should only look out for yourself. And some believe you should never give, only take.

I've found that those who only look out for themselves usually end up by themselves.

Playing sports has shown me the magic of being part of something bigger than one person.

Ben VanHouten

Surrender Me for We

Being on a team makes you see things differently.

Everyone on a team brings their own special skills and everyone has a role.

When you stick together and pull for each other, you know everyone has your back. You pick each other up. Teamwork makes all work easier.

Sharing experiences together sweetens the victories and helps ease painful losses.

When you're on a team that's working together, you forget about yourself and your statistics.

You give up the *me* for *we*.

Teammates have four nicknames for Mike: "Cam," "Cammy," "Spiderman" (for his wall climbing), and the "Comet" (for his speed).

After the game my teammates all shared in my excitement by giving me the royal treatment. They wrapped a bat in foil, taped together towels for a robe, and made a cardboard crown that said "King Cam." Dressed as a king, I walked under a salute of bats over my head.

Ben VanHouten

Five days later the Mariners celebrated my four home runs by giving me a plaque before a home game.

An Unforgettable Night

I thought about more than myself on May 2, 2002, as I stood in Chicago's chilly Comiskey Park, one swing away from a legendary baseball record.

In 126 years of games no player has ever hit five home runs in a major league game. A dozen guys have "gone yard" four times.

That night I was in an amazing zone. I hit four homers in my first four at-bats. In the ninth inning I worked the count to three balls, no strikes. We were winning big, so some might have frowned on me swinging on a 3–0 count.

I didn't want to do anything to disrespect my teammates, the other team, or the game, even if it cost me the record. So I took a perfect fastball down the middle. I did get my chance to swing for five. I fouled off a pitch and then hit a line drive to right field that was caught just in front of the fence.

Hitting four in a row blew my mind. I never do that, even in batting practice. Teammate Bret Boone and I did write history in the first inning when we hit two home runs each back-to-back!

That night is the most thrilling thing that's happened to me in baseball so far. Ironically, I came into the game carrying a hitting slump.

That's what's so cool about sports. You never know when something special is going to happen.

The Mariners Lose Three Superstars

Nobody could have guessed how special the 2001 Seattle Mariners would be when we started our workouts in spring training.

The Mariner organization had lost three superstars, one in each of the previous three years: Randy Johnson, Ken Griffey Jr., and Alex Rodriguez.

Some writers picked us to finish second in the American League West. Others said we'd finish last.

I always have a positive frame of mind and think that good things are going to happen, but even I didn't dream of what was to come. No one did.

Teamwork Is the Key

We truly became an international team in 2001, with guys from the United States, the Dominican Republic, Puerto Rico, Venezuela, and Japan. We had a good mix of young players and veterans.

There were new faces at key positions, including a 5'9" mystery player named Ichiro Suzuki.

From this group a new team emerged whose winning ways had not been matched in 94 years of professional baseball.

The 2001 Mariners won 116 regular-season games, tying the record set by the 1906 Chicago Cubs.

From the players to the front-office staff, each member of the Mariner organization will tell you the secret to our success can be summed up in one word: teamwork.

AP/Wide World Photos

My Favorite Team

"When Mike was a baby he had to wear a bar on his feet [corrective shoes connected by a metal bar] at night to straighten his feet because they were so pigeon-toed."
—Janice, Mike's mother

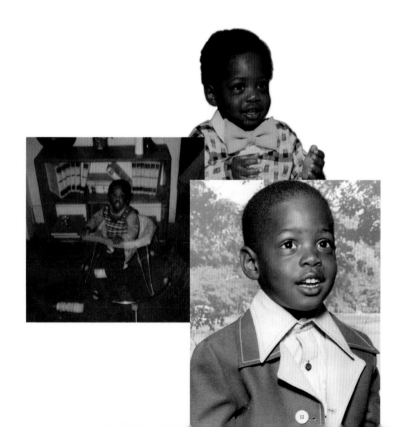

Before I go any further, however, I need to tell you about the teamwork that helped me make it to the major leagues.

My family needed teamwork to raise me because when I was born (on January 8, 1973), my father and mother weren't ready to get married or care for a newborn baby.

So my grandmother, who had already raised nine children of her own, adopted me. I grew up in the same modest, four-bedroom house where my mother spent her childhood in LaGrange, Georgia.

Once a year, I rent a bus and treat my extended family to one of my team's East Coast series. Any family of 50 that can survive a three-day bus trip together has to be tight . . . and mine is.

Jimmy Thornton
My father served in the army after high school and later returned to LaGrange, where he works in a machine–parts factory. He played adult competitive softball for many years.

Janice Cameron
My mother stayed in LaGrange and works at the same carpet factory where my grand–mother and grandfather worked.

Fannie M. Cameron
My grandmother grew up on a share–cropper's farm and worked in a carpet factory for most of her life.

I can tell you straight up that I never felt ashamed or strange about my family situation.

My grandmother, who I call Mama, gave me love, support, and firm guidance.

Even though my mother and father never married each other and built their own separate families, I had the best of both worlds.

They lived a few miles away and stayed involved in my life. Instead of one family, I really had three. It takes a team to raise a child.

I'm grateful my family didn't fight over me. They worked together for me.

"Mike always loved sports. When he was real small, I bought him a plastic bat and ball. He loved to play ball. He'd play ball all day. I never dreamed he'd be a major league player."
—Fannie M. Cameron, Mike's grandmother

My grandmother's house, where I grew up.

"All those acrobatic diving catches you see Mike make in center field—he made those same catches in our neighborhood street games. To play baseball, we used wood or plastic bats or broom sticks or tree branches. He never really dominated any one sport. He was always kind of skinny. He always had power and that extra burst. He's always been a hard worker and team player. If there was an argument, he'd let you have your way. He was always a good athlete and a great person and still is. He hasn't changed a bit."
—Travis Moore, longtime friend

Homes in my neighborhood weren't big. Yet they were full of kids eager to play games. What I remember most about growing up is playing sports in the streets and fields around my house. We played whatever sport was in season—football, basketball, or baseball.

Even though I was one of the smaller kids, I learned to compete on our streets. We'd go all out to win. We'd play for hours and challenge kids from nearby neighborhoods. Playing sports kept us out of trouble.

I fell in love with sports. My bedroom walls held posters of Dr. J, Terry Bradshaw, and Rickey Henderson.

The street in front of my childhood home, where we played thousands of games.

A Hair-Raising Experience

On sweltering summer afternoons, only the bells of the ice-cream truck stopped us from our outdoor games.

I always had some change in my pockets and often bought ice cream for my friends. Some thought my grandmother spoiled me by giving me an allowance ($20 dollars a week in elementary school).

I did earn some money by being the neighborhood barber. I started experimenting with cutting friends' hair and word spread of my new talent. Soon long lines of kids would form at my house for a haircut. It got so out of hand that I started charging a little for the cuts.

"Mike always had money with him. When the ice-cream man came, Mike would buy you what you wanted and say you could pay him back later. If he went to McDonald's, he'd ask if you wanted something. If he had fries and you didn't, he'd share with you—even down to the last fry, he'd split it with you."

—Travis Moore, longtime friend

A Favorite Christmas Gift

A Christmas gift really made me famous in my neighborhood one year.

For more than a year I had my heart set on it. Mama told me if I was good, maybe I'd get it. I couldn't believe my eyes when I saw the cherry-red go-cart in front of the Christmas tree.

I drove that go-cart all around the fields near my house. In the eyes of my friends, I had the perfect sports car.

My first real car, however, was a different story.

I wrecked my Toyota Celica during a freak winter storm that iced the roads during my high school days. Someone stopped suddenly and I slid into them. Another car hit me from behind. Fortunately, nobody was hurt.

Years before I got my go-cart, this plastic car made me smile on Christmas morning.

Everyone Else Is Doing It

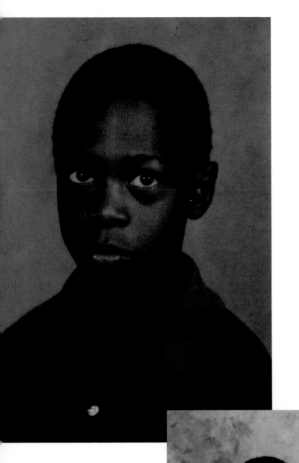

I caused a few head-on collisions in class with my teachers. I had one problem: I talked too much.

Through elementary school, junior high, and the start of high school, I got in trouble for talking.

Teachers called in my grandmother for conferences.

"Why do you talk so much in class?" Mama would ask. "I can't believe it, because you don't hardly talk at all at home."

I used the same excuse all kids use: "I can't help it, Mama, everybody else is doing it."

No matter where I sat in class, a friend was close by. When someone talked to me, I answered.

I wasn't the class clown and I wasn't disrespectful. I just couldn't figure out the appropriate times to talk.

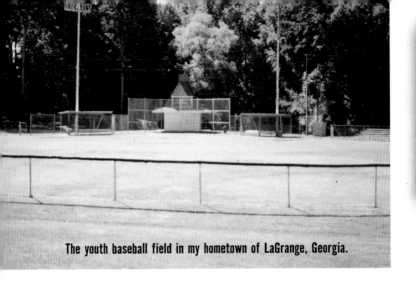
The youth baseball field in my hometown of LaGrange, Georgia.

"Watching him grow up, he never was the best player. People aren't born to be major leaguers; you have to work hard to get there. We're all proud of what he's accomplished because we never thought he'd be at the level he is."

—Jimmy Thornton, Mike's father

Not making the All-Star baseball team when I was 11 really confused me.

My father and coaches will tell you I wasn't the best player in our youth leagues. OK, maybe I wasn't. But I could pitch, and I played a mean shortstop (which is where I secretly wish I could play now). I had pop in my bat. I hit about 10 home runs as a 12-year-old.

So for all those who don't make All-Star teams, don't sweat it. I know how it feels. One year I didn't make an All-Star team, either. Don't give up on yourself. I didn't.

"From ages six to eleven, I don't remember losing a game until plums cost us a victory. Halfway into a game, I was pitching a shutout. On the mound my stomach started to churn. I felt like I was going to throw up. So I took myself out of the game and we lost. Turns out I ate a handful of plums before the game and that upset my stomach."

—Mike

Curveballs

Whenever I played youth sports, I always had the biggest rooting section because I had three families cheering me.

17

A World Series Victory

I kept growing my game and finally started getting my props.

I made the area All-Star team for 15-year-olds and competed in a "World Series" in Texarkana, Texas.

Playing against teams from all over the country showed me it doesn't matter where you come from. What matters is how you compete on the field.

We competed well and brought home the championship.

My basketball coach forced me to pick either hoops or baseball after ninth grade. It wasn't a tough choice.

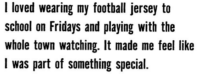

I loved wearing my football jersey to school on Fridays and playing with the whole town watching. It made me feel like I was part of something special.

A Three-Sport Athlete

By the time I got to high school, the coaches knew my name. I played three sports—football, basketball, and baseball—in ninth grade. Our ninth-grade basketball team was terrible. We had a 1–8 record.

I almost didn't turn out for football my sophomore year, but our coach drove by my house and personally asked me to play, so I did. I played cornerback and wide receiver and earned some playing time on the varsity team.

A painful thing happened during my junior season. I broke my left wrist making a tackle. I stayed in for two more plays before I realized it was broken. I played with a cast the next week.

My high school's nickname is the "Grangers." It means farmers.

As you can see, I looked like a boy playing among young men during my sophomore year. People teased me about being short and slender. Some even mentioned it in my school yearbook.

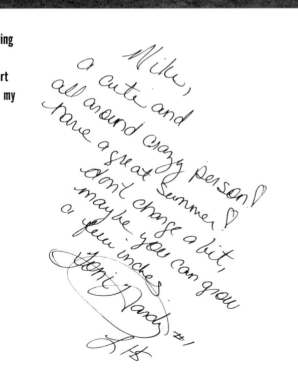

Mike,
a cute and all around crazy person! Have a great summer! don't change a bit, maybe you can grow a few inches.
Homi Nardy #1
L+S

A Boy Among Men

I was afraid that my damaged wrist would threaten my junior baseball season.

For weeks after football ended, my wrist ached. I had nightmares about sitting out the season. That injury seemed like the end of the world to me.

But as the baseball season neared, my wrist healed quickly.

I made the varsity team as a sophomore and played some at third base and pitched. I felt I opened some eyes and gained confidence.

My junior year would be my coming out party. Or so I thought.

Flunking Chemistry

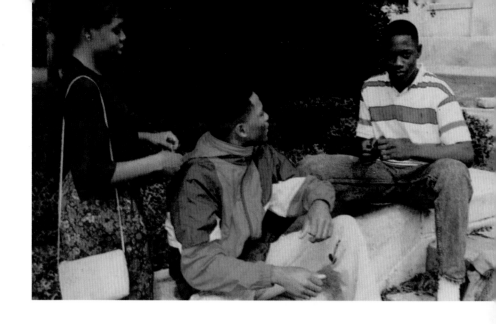

I lifted weights and added muscle to my growing body. I worked on my baseball skills and improved.

But I had trouble in my junior year chemistry class. I asked the teacher for extra help and a chance to do extra credit. I studied hard and did the best I could. Still, I fell short.

At my school at that time, grades were A, B, C, and F. When athletes failed a class, they had to sit out the next season.

I missed a C in chemistry by one point during the winter. One stinkin' point!

So I sat out my entire junior baseball season.

It embarrassed and frustrated me.

"I taught Mike for three years. When Mike was a freshman, he was a skinny runt of a kid. He talked all the time. Over three years I saw a lot of growth and maturity. By the time he was a junior in my geometry class, he was the perfect student. He was goal oriented and knew exactly what he wanted to do with his life."

—Francee Mitchell, LaGrange High School math teacher

Figuring It Out

Jabreka and Mike on prom night.

Looking back, missing that season forced me to work harder than ever before. I took care of business in school and worked out every day to prepare for baseball.

It showed me that playing sports is a privilege, not a guarantee.

I found that the only thing worse than not playing is not being on a team.

Many people helped me through that rough spot. Family, friends, and coaches all encouraged me not to give up.

A girl at my school kept me from going crazy. Hanging out with her eased my mind. Jabreka, my first and only real girlfriend, showed me that there is life outside of sports. We started dating my junior year and we've been together ever since.

"He's a very good father to our three kids. He's kind-hearted, has a good sense of humor, and is an honest person. What else can I say?"
—Jabreka Cameron, Mike's wife

"Mike is like the brother I never had. He used to come over and wash our cars in high school. He is so sweet. He always has something nice to say about everyone."
—Tawase, Mike's sister-in-law

Mike and Jabreka's children (from top): daughter Tája and sons Dazmon and Mekhi.

An MVP Senior Season

LaGrange High had only one winning baseball season before Mike joined the program. During his senior year the team went to the state playoffs and finished 21–6. Mike's stats as a senior: .403 batting average, three home runs, 25 RBI, two saves, and a 2.00 ERA.

"Mike did whatever it took to help the team win. As a senior, Mike was forced to pitch to give us a chance to win a championship. He wasn't a pitcher, but he was a competitor. He had a strong arm, and he went out and battled and won a lot of games for us."
—Donnie Branch, LaGrange High School baseball coach

During my senior season the team needed my speed in the outfield more than they did in the infield, so I switched to center field. I wasn't happy about it at first. I wanted my shot at shortstop. But in team situations, sometimes you have to swallow your own desires and play where the coach thinks you'll help the most. I also pitched in on the mound.

Seems like whenever scouts were at our games, I played well. I didn't hit many home runs, mostly doubles. Despite not having any playoff tradition, we advanced to the state playoffs. We made it to the semifinals before losing in a strange way.

With the winning run on third, our pitcher accidentally dropped the baseball while standing on the mound taking signs from the catcher. The umpires correctly ruled it a balk. The runner scored. Game over. Everyone felt crushed. We all came together and told our pitcher not to worry about it—that we were all a team, win or lose.

I finally caught up with the other kids physically by my senior season.

23

LaGrange Daily News

Cameron Signs With White Sox

By RONNIE SIVELL
Daily News Sports Writer

LaGrange High's outstanding center fielder Mike Cameron has signed a professional contract with the Chicago White Sox.

The 6-foot-1, 170-pound outfielder was drafted in the 14th round of last week's amateur draft and has left for Sarasota in the Rookie League.

Cameron batted .403 with three home runs this season for the Grangers and drove in 25 runs. He was also used in a relief pitching role and registered two saves for the Grangers with a 2.00 ERA.

But it was Cameron's play in center field that caught the major league scouts' attention.

"Mike has a great work ethic and attitude," Granger baseball coach Donnie Branch said.

"He has a great arm and possesses good speed. He also has a big-time bat, so he has all the skills that major league scouts

Mike Cameron

League.

Cameron would like to join two other members of the Chicago White Sox who have local ties.

First baseman Frank Thomas played at Columbus High before going to Auburn and Warren Newsome who played at Newnan has just recently been called up to the majors from the White Sox' triple-A team in Vancouver of the Pacific Coast League.

Cameron named his grandmother Fannie Cameron, his father Jimmy Thornton, along with LaGrange coaches Donnie Branch and Jon Powell, youth [...] and White Sox [...]

Drafted!

My high school baseball coach will tell you I wasn't the best hitter on our team, but the professional scouts saw potential in me.

The Chicago White Sox drafted me in round 14 of the 1991 draft, making me the first player chosen by a professional baseball team from LaGrange High School.

After graduation, my grandmother wanted me to go to college instead of being a pro baseball player. She even talked to a lawyer about forcing me to go to college. But we talked it out. I convinced her baseball was my best option.

> "Mike was a complete player, but he wasn't one of the best hitters we've ever had at LaGrange. He made himself a great hitter through hard work and determination."
> —Donnie Branch, LaGrange High School baseball coach

Learning the Ropes

CHICAGO WHITE SOX 1991

Gaines Du Vall Sports Portraits

Suited up for my first season in professional baseball.

I played for six full seasons on six different teams in the minor leagues. Two highlights came during my first and third spring-training camps.

That's when I teamed with two of the greatest athletes ever: Bo Jackson and Michael Jordan.

I learned much by just watching how they carried themselves and interacted with teammates.

Bo, a rare two-sport professional athlete who played for three different major league baseball teams and the Raiders of the NFL, attempted a courageous comeback after injuring his hip while playing football. With a replaced hip, he played for the White Sox and the Angels. He went out and competed every day in spring training. He gave everything he had. In sports, that's all anyone can ask.

Bo stuttered, yet he wasn't afraid to talk. He knew how to keep the clubhouse loose by joking around. He never felt sorry for himself. Bo could laugh through his pain. He stayed positive even when things weren't going well for him.

AP/Wide World Photos

Bo Jackson.

It's easy to be a great teammate when things are going your way. The true test is how you react when things don't go your way. Watching Bo cope with his struggle inspired me.

Baby-Blue Jordans

Michael Jordan, the most famous athlete of my time, had a dream of playing two pro sports, like Bo. You have to admire him. He gave it a shot.

Michael never acted like he was better than anyone while playing minor league baseball for the White Sox. The best basketball player in the world never acted like he was better than anyone. He was just one of the guys. He was humble and asked lots of questions about how to be a better baseball player.

Most of all, he enjoyed competing.

One day during spring training, he made me a promise: "If you hit two home runs in a game, I'll have a pair of my new shoes in your locker the next morning," he said.

Sure enough, one game I knocked it out twice. The next day, before 8:00 A.M., a pair of baby-blue Michael Jordan shoes appeared in my locker. I couldn't believe it.

Minor League Highlights

On the field, my favorite minor league season came in 1993, when we won our league championship. Any title is worth celebrating.

I grabbed headlines during the 1996 season in Birmingham, Alabama, with a run at becoming the first minor leaguer to go 30/30 (30 home runs, 30 stolen bases). I missed it by two, as I finished with 28 home runs and 39 stolen bases. I hit .300 and started making a name for myself.

Mike throws and bats right-handed, but he is ambidextrous, which means he can use both hands equally.

My Darkest Day

My scariest moment in the minors came when I almost lost an eye in 1995.

While I was shagging fly balls during batting practice, a ball dropped toward me. Just then, a pitcher ran in front of me. I lost sight of the ball and it hit me smack in the right eye and broke my eye socket. I couldn't see for two weeks. It terrified me.

Slowly, my sight returned. I'm still sensitive to strong light, which is why I wear sunglasses all the time.

"He's always willing to cheer up a teammate. He's very support-ive. He's a good family man and a good all-around person. He's a perfect pupil. I love working with him. He's always coming out to do the extra stuff to make himself a better player."
—Gerald Perry, Mariners hitting coach

Ben VanHouten

Jamie Squire/Getty Images

One Tough Job

An eye-opening experience happened during an off-season while I was still in the minors. I needed some extra money, so I got a job working at an aluminum factory. During high school, I had worked in a hotel doing maintenance, but I had never before worked as hard as I did at that factory.

I worked from 6:00 A.M. to 6:00 P.M. making aluminum rolls and putting them in boxes. That was tough.

The experience gave me new respect for my grandmother and parents and all the jobs they've worked to help me have a better life.

My dad always used to say: "Whatever you do, make sure you enjoy what you do."

Whenever I'm a little down about baseball, thinking about working in that factory makes me realize how fortunate I am to be paid for what I love to do.

> "He plays the game like a kid in the backyard. There's this youthful spirit that comes out in him. Kirby Puckett had it, too. Cammy always has a smile on his face. He reminds us baseball is supposed to be fun."
> —Rick Rizzs,
> Mariners broadcaster

Ready or Not

I broke into the major leagues in 1995 when the White Sox called me up at the end of the season. I did OK, with seven hits in 38 at-bats, and even hit my first big-league homer.

The next year I had that great season in Birmingham, hitting .300. When the White Sox called me up, however, I did worse than I had the year before. I had just one hit in 11 tries.

I started the 1997 season in Nashville, the team's AAA club, and got off to a strong start.

The White Sox called me up during the season and I've been in the majors ever since.

I posted solid numbers—14 homers, 55 RBI, and a .259 batting average. I started believing some of the media stories about my potential. I got a little bigheaded after the season. I slacked off in my workouts.

As a result, I fell into a horrible slump and lost my starting job the next season. I finished with just a .210 batting average.

I placed many late-night phone calls to Jabreka and my dad that season. They kept me from feeling sorry for myself. White Sox slugger Frank Thomas took me under his wing and kept pumping me up.

I learned that when you're down, you shouldn't try to go it alone. Reach out to those close to you for help. Then lift up others when you get the chance.

Mike and his relatives pose with Frank Thomas after a game.

Jonathan Daniel/Getty Images

Otto Greule Jr./Getty Images

Reality Bites

I regrouped mentally during the winter and renewed my commitment to being the best player I could be. That's when I started shaving my head to remind myself that I needed to work hard every day.

I played winter baseball that year in the Dominican Republic. There a triple whammy hit me—boom, boom, boom.

First, I came down with stomach flu—the kind that makes you feel like your stomach is coming out your mouth.

A few days later, I messed up my shoulder when I collided with an infielder as we ran for a fly ball.

Then my agent, Mike Nicotera, called to tell me that the White Sox had traded me to Cincinnati. The management didn't even respect me enough to call and tell me.

I felt betrayed.

Ben VanHouten

Lou Piniella.

"First of all, he's a great athlete, a real five-tool player. There's nothing he can't do. And in the clubhouse, he's a guy the other players look to and learn from. He's a real positive guy, very upbeat."
—Lou Piniella, Mariners manager

Filling My Own Shoes

It took a while to get over that incident and to understand that baseball is a business.

But I made friends fast in Cincinnati, especially with Greg Vaughn.

Just when I felt comfortable after my second season with the Reds, I got traded again, this time for one of the best outfielders in history, Ken Griffey Jr.

I heard about it while working out at my old high school in the offseason.

My head swirled with thoughts. I started feeling the pressure of living up to Griffey.

I didn't know much about Seattle. I heard Lou Piniella could be tough on young players and that worried me.

Lou called me two hours later and said, "Go out and play and everything's going to be OK. Do what you're capable of doing. We have other guys who will take up the slack."

That was just what I needed to hear and was also a great lesson.

It showed me that what you hear about people isn't always true. In team situations, start each relationship with an open mind and only worry about filling your own shoes.

First Impressions

I had an open mind about Seattle, but I started hearing that Seattle didn't have an open mind about me.

I heard some fans and media people saying that Seattle didn't get anything in the trade for Junior. Along with myself, three others came to Seattle in the deal.

It motivated me when people said I was nothing.

Teammates greeted me with open arms in spring training, especially Jay Buhner.

When someone new joins your team, be sure to welcome him or her. You only have one chance at a first impression.

I felt I needed to make a solid first showing in Seattle. My first game at Safeco Field made me feel like I had fallen on my face. I went 0-for-4 with three strikeouts. That was against Boston's dominating pitcher Pedro Martinez, so I didn't get too down on myself.

> "He wasn't taking over for Griffey. He didn't worry about people's expectations. People fall into that trap. He was mature enough to handle that situation and went out to try to be Mike Cameron."
> —Mark McLemore, Mariners utility player

Ben VanHouten

Finding My Groove

In our next series, with the New York Yankees, Seattle fans surprised me with a two-minute standing ovation before I batted. I felt overwhelmed. It was a community hug, as if they were all saying, "It's OK, Mike. We know you can do it."

Supportive fans do make a difference to pro players.

That weekend I made a leaping catch off the wall, robbing Derek Jeter of a home run. I could almost hear skeptical fans breathing a sigh of relief.

I proved I could play the game during the rest of the season and was proud of my first season in Seattle.

AP/Wide World Photos

AP/Wide World Photos

"I think all the pitchers here like having him out there in center field. He's going to catch the ball if you give him a chance, even balls over the wall."
—Freddy Garcia, Mariners pitcher

AP/Wide World Photos

Otton Greule Jr./Getty Images

Sweet Celebration

The end of the 2000 season proved intense because we had to win a lot of games down the stretch to make the playoffs.

Ironically, my first playoff experience came against the team I started with—the White Sox. I didn't carry a grudge for how they had treated me, but when Carlos Guillen bunted Rickey Henderson home to knock out Chicago, it was extra special for me.

Instead of celebrating in the clubhouse, most of us came out to share our enjoyment with our fans. I poured champagne on myself and some fans, and I even wore a silly looking foam M on my head.

Although the Yankees ousted us in the American League Championship Series, everyone felt that the team had made progress.

Pass the Encouragement

The Mike Cameron batting cage.

Ben VanHouten

While I progressed from the minors to the big leagues, I often went back to my high school during winter months to work out and talk with the young athletes.

Several years ago I mentioned to coach Branch that I wanted to do something to improve the baseball facilities at the school. We came up with a plan and found some matching funds to go with my donation. Together an indoor batting cage was built and the baseball field and stands were upgraded.

Baseball has given me many opportunities to reach out to others. Whether I'm speaking to a group of kids or signing autographs before a game, the most important thing I can give to people is encouragement. I want people to know that I'm just a regular guy whose accomplishments prove that hard work does pay off.

> "He's a very genuine person. He cares about people. When he asks you how you are doing, he means it. He's one of those guys everyone likes, even the opposing team . . . maybe not the pitchers."
>
> —Mark McLemore

- Mike has joined with the state of Washington to promote awareness of positive fatherhood through public service announcements.
- Cameron also teamed with the National Center for Fathering to honor winners of a "Father of the Year" writing essay.
- Mike donated funds to help build an indoor batting facility at his alma mater, LaGrange High School (pictured above).
- When the LaGrange High football team advanced to the state playoffs in 2001 and suddenly needed new turf shoes, Mike donated funds to purchase new shoes for the entire team.
- Mike has created the Cam4Kids foundation to raise funds for established children's programs.

Rice Is Nice

Before the 2001 season, I traveled to Seattle for the February Fanfest. There, I met Ichiro Suzuki in the Safeco batting cage. I watched him hit and instantly knew that this seven-time Japanese batting champ would be a star in the States. We introduced ourselves.

"I saw you play on TV a few times last year. Nice to meet you," said Ichiro, who can speak some English.

During spring training we developed a strong friendship. I call him "Ichy." He calls me "Cam." Besides playing next to each other in the outfield, our clubhouse lockers are side by side.

AP/Wide World Photos

"Mike has good leadership, making us relax and laugh. He is an excellent mood maker. He has been very kind to me since I joined this organization. He always talks to me in the clubhouse, and he's open-armed to take me in and make me feel comfortable like home. All those things make Mike a very good teammate."
—Ichiro Suzuki, Mariners outfielder

Ichiro definitely does some things differently than most American players. His swing is strange—he's almost running as he hits. He's stretching all the time. He has this stick he uses to massage his feet. And he eats rice balls before games.

Ichiro's favorite pregame snack. Riceballs are made of sea vegetables and rice wrapped in seaweed.

A Hot Start

Bret Boone and I decided early on that if it worked for Ichy, we'd try the rice balls. Ichiro's wife made us one before almost every home game.

One thing you don't do in baseball is mess with a streak. Our team started off sizzling, winning 20 of our first 25 games. So Bret and I kept eating the rice balls.

Winning is contagious. After winning a string of games in the late innings, fans came up with the saying: "Two Outs, So What?"

Every night a different hero emerged. Our team clicked, on and off the field.

"When someone is not trying hard and disrespecting the game, that's the biggest cancer to a team. Mike plays hard and respects the game."
—Stan Javier,
Mariners outfielder, 2000–2001

Singing Center Fielder

One tradition I started helps with team unity. Whenever we travel on our team bus, I always sing. I grab the microphone and belt out my favorite Michael Jackson song, "Working Day and Night."

Then, I'll give a shout out of praise to teammates. I'll call out players and acknowledge everyone who had a good week. The bus busts up with laughter as guys throw out clever one-liners.

Another thing I like to do is to create sayings and put them on T-shirts. One of my first in Seattle was: "Enjoy my enjoyment."

Others were: "Do what you do" and "What's going on around this place?"

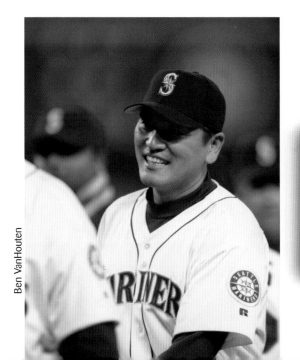

Ben VanHouten

"When people are down, he cheers everyone up. He starts singing on the bus. He's not as good of a singer as me."
—Kazuhiro Sasaki, Mariners pitcher

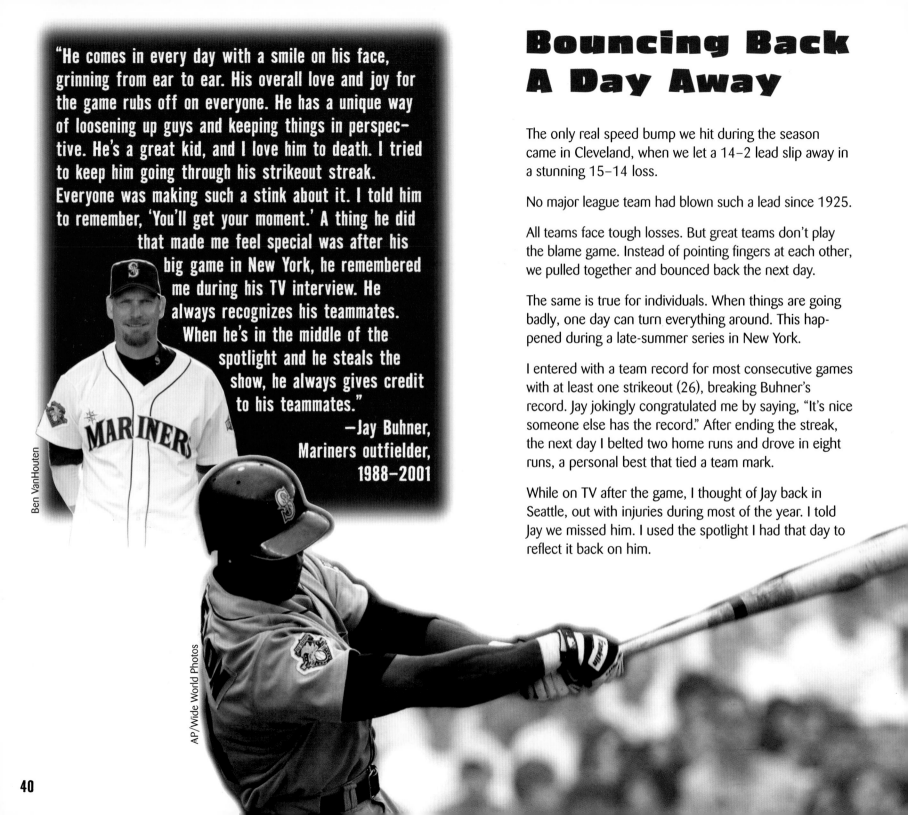

"He comes in every day with a smile on his face, grinning from ear to ear. His overall love and joy for the game rubs off on everyone. He has a unique way of loosening up guys and keeping things in perspective. He's a great kid, and I love him to death. I tried to keep him going through his strikeout streak. Everyone was making such a stink about it. I told him to remember, 'You'll get your moment.' A thing he did that made me feel special was after his big game in New York, he remembered me during his TV interview. He always recognizes his teammates. When he's in the middle of the spotlight and he steals the show, he always gives credit to his teammates."

—Jay Buhner,
Mariners outfielder,
1988–2001

Ben VanHouten

AP/Wide World Photos

Bouncing Back A Day Away

The only real speed bump we hit during the season came in Cleveland, when we let a 14–2 lead slip away in a stunning 15–14 loss.

No major league team had blown such a lead since 1925.

All teams face tough losses. But great teams don't play the blame game. Instead of pointing fingers at each other, we pulled together and bounced back the next day.

The same is true for individuals. When things are going badly, one day can turn everything around. This happened during a late-summer series in New York.

I entered with a team record for most consecutive games with at least one strikeout (26), breaking Buhner's record. Jay jokingly congratulated me by saying, "It's nice someone else has the record." After ending the streak, the next day I belted two home runs and drove in eight runs, a personal best that tied a team mark.

While on TV after the game, I thought of Jay back in Seattle, out with injuries during most of the year. I told Jay we missed him. I used the spotlight I had that day to reflect it back on him.

My Biggest Surprise

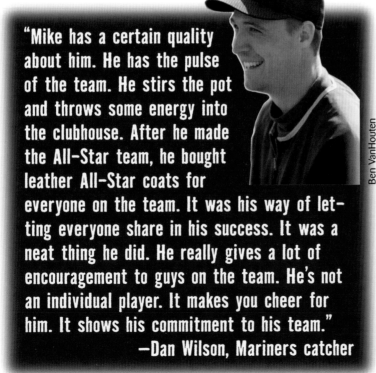

Ben VanHouten

Mike earned his first Gold Glove award in 2001 as one of the top three outfielders in the American League.

Mike and his son Dazmon.

"Mike has a certain quality about him. He has the pulse of the team. He stirs the pot and throws some energy into the clubhouse. After he made the All-Star team, he bought leather All-Star coats for everyone on the team. It was his way of letting everyone share in his success. It was a neat thing he did. He really gives a lot of encouragement to guys on the team. He's not an individual player. It makes you cheer for him. It shows his commitment to his team."
—Dan Wilson, Mariners catcher

Ben VanHouten

An old friend unknowingly allowed me to be a part of baseball's All-Star spotlight. An injury prevented Greg Vaughn from playing, so I was chosen to take his place in the 2001 All-Star Game, hosted in Seattle.

I heard about it in Los Angeles right before I was to bat in the middle of a game. My body tingled, and I shed a tear of excitement. I promptly hit into a double play.

What made it more special was that I wanted to take my son Dazmon (four at the time) to the All-Star home-run contest and let him hang out on the field. When I found out you had to be on the All-Star team to be on the field, I started asking every Mariner official if they could make an exception for me and Dazmon. But they all said that's the rule.

When Lee Pelekoudas, a vice president for the Mariners, pulled me into the tunnel before my at-bat, I immediately thought something was wrong with my family—the house was burning down or someone was sick.

"You don't have to worry about taking your son on the field for the All-Star Game for the home-run derby," he said. "You'll be there for three days. You're going to the All-Star Game."

A Day in the Sun

When we returned to Safeco that night on the team bus, I walked into the clubhouse to see all the names of the game's best players on the lockers, mine included. I tried on my All-Star jersey, feeling a bubbling of excitement. I couldn't help giggling: "I'm an All-Star!"

Dazmon and I had a fun-filled day watching the home-run contest. I just wanted to drink up the whole weekend experience.

Standing on the foul line and being introduced as an All-Star is something I'll always cherish. Midway into the game, I lined a singled to left-center. I was so thrilled, I just kept running and stretched it into a double.

For one day, at least, I felt like I was one of the best players in baseball.

Ben VanHouten

Ben VanHouten

"He does take his business seriously. He's one of the hardest workers on the team. When things go wrong, you don't have to take it too seriously. You have to relax and make fun of yourself."

—Edgar Martinez,
Mariners designated hitter

Ben VanHouten

"Everyone has a day when they need someone to pick them up. There have been times that I've picked him up and times he's picked me up. On this team, everyone's in tune with everyone else and knows when someone is down. Sometimes to pick someone up it can be a word, or a pat on the back, or sitting on the plane sharing music or doing a crossword puzzle together."
—Mark McLemore

September 11

The darkest day of the season came September 11 on our last trip of the season to Anaheim. A phone call from Jabreka woke me up.

"Mike, turn on the TV, quick!"

I did and witnessed the terrorist attack on the Twin Towers unfolding. I was in shock when I saw the second plane slam into the tower. A burning feeling fell over me.

A lot of the guys on the team were in disarray. Lou Piniella took it the hardest. He spent many seasons in New York. People didn't know what to do. Everyone wanted to be home with their families, but because planes were grounded, we were stuck there for a few days.

Ben VanHouten

United

I've heard our national anthem before games about a million times. But, I'm telling you, in that first game back the song had new meaning.

When we clinched the American League West title, we wanted to be respectful of what happened in New York. Mark McLemore spontaneously grabbed the U.S. flag as the team marched around the infield. We stopped on the mound and fell to our knees and prayed.

For those two nights I felt a new unity as I had never felt before. One nation. One world.

> "He has no enemies on the team. He gets along with everyone."
> —Charles Gipson, Mariners outfielder

Playoff Courage

The events of September 11 put baseball, and all of sports, in perspective. There are more important things.

Still, we all knew we couldn't let terrorists take baseball away.

Even though we didn't make it to the World Series, our team showed tremendous courage in the playoffs.

After losing Game 1 to Cleveland, we hung together and rallied despite mounting pressure.

We bounced back in Game 2 for a 5–1 win with home runs by Edgar Martinez and myself in the first inning. When I hit my two-run shot, Booney met me at home and laughingly said, "You stink!"

We lost the next game 17–2 and were one loss away from elimination. But we took the next two must-win games to claim the hard-fought series.

Next, we faced the Yankees again in the American League Championship Series. The winner would go to the World Series.

AP/Wide World Photos

"I really enjoy playing with him. The thing I most respect is when I walk into the clubhouse, I don't know if he's gone 12-for-15 or 0-for-15. He's the same whether he's on a hot streak or a cold streak. He's very professional in that way."

—Bret Boone,
Mariners
second baseman

AP/Wide World Photos

AP/Wide World Photos

Falling to the Yankees

New York had the emotional edge with most of the country pulling for them.

We dropped the first two at home, won the next game in New York, and almost tied the series in Game 4. But our 1–0 lead slipped away with two dramatic Yankee homers in the last two innings.

A win there and the series would have been forced back to Seattle. That might have changed the outcome.

The next night, I believed in my heart that we could come back. But the truth is our offense fell short in the series, my hitting included, and we were knocked out.

Baseball is a very crazy game. The best regular-season team doesn't always win in the play-offs. It's the team that's playing the best in the postseason. New York played a little better.

AP/Wide World Photos

I sat in the dugout, dazed, after making the last out of the season. I couldn't believe our magic ride was over.

A Season to Remember

It took a few days to shake off the disappointment of falling short of our World Series goal. Now, however, when I think of our 2001 season, I remember all we accomplished together.

We all learned that we need to count on each other more than ever.

And the Mariners proved that, no matter what you do, it *does* take a team.

Mike's Young Fans on Teamwork

"On a winning team you have to have a group of people that is willing to give all of what they have for their team. Usually that means that people are getting along and are close to each other. So many people worry about themselves and what everyone else might think about them. People that are close are going to work better together to drive toward what they want. The unsuccessful teams usually have people that have resentful feelings toward someone on the team. It takes a team to reach a dream."

—Bryce Bircher, age 13, Redmond, WA

"It takes a team to survive. If you were alone on an island surviving in the wild, you would have the title of living, but you wouldn't really be alive because you wouldn't feel there was a purpose to life. Others supply you with the strength and love that you need to survive. Without this support, humans tend to feel lost, unusual, and incomplete. It takes a team of people to keep its members alive."

—Clarissa Barrett, age 13, Marcellus, NY

"Sometimes you have to do what's right. Like when you and your brothers and sisters have to clean up, it takes all of y'all to work as a team. That's what it means to me—you have to do it together."

—Ebonee Towns, age 12, LaGrange, GA

"Teamwork is hard work. But it feels good when you help your team."

—Lars Wollum, age 4, Auburn, WA

"Teamwork is all working together without any superstars because we're all superstars."

—Katie Carroll, age 8, Yakima, WA

"Team work is something that you need to do.
It can't be done by only you.
With your friends you play the game.
After the event you feel the same.
If you lose or if you win
your team will be there with a happy grin.
Working by yourself is sad and lonely,
but with a team it is warm and homey.
So be a team and work together,
through sunny and rainy weather.
And in the long run you will find
that being a team is always on your mind."

—Kelsey Wilson, age 15, Surrey, British Columbia